AMERICAN MAGIC

Gil Kofman

BROADWAY PLAY PUBLISHING INC
New York
www.broadwayplaypublishing.com
info@broadwayplaypublishing.com

AMERICAN MAGIC
© Copyright 2008 by Gil Kofman

Cover art by Nathan Fox
First printing: August 2008
I S B N: 978-0-88145-392-8

Book design: Marie Donovan
Word processing: Microsoft Word
Typographic controls: Ventura Publisher
Typeface: Palatino

The original production of AMERICAN MAGIC was produced by Shock@Awe Productions at Altered Stages in N Y C in May 2003. It later moved to Los Angeles at 2100 Sq. Feet for June/July 2003 with same cast.

MAN ....Indrajit Sarkar
RON .... Sonny Perez
DON .... Walter Murray
WOMAN ....Lyndsay Rose Kane

VOICE OF PRESIDENT ....Richard Foreman

Director ....Matthew Wilder
Music .... Lee Ranaldo

A more recent production was done at the Hen and Chickens Theater in London UK.

CHARACTERS & SETTING

MAN, *Indian mind reader*
RON, *Secret Service man, all business, short fuse at times*
DON, *Secret Service man, has a son, likes to meditate*
WOMAN, *Secret Service, at top of the power triangle, sultry, calculating*
PRESIDENT'S VOICE, *only heard, never seen*

Time: a time of fear, when the masses are easily swayed and manipulated by convenient government alerts and easily programmed xenophobia.

dedicated to Amy Ziering
who believed even in doubt

Scene 1

(Spotlight on MAN *in a fancy pair of silk pajamas, a colorful turban on his head. He mingles with audience as they enter. Very histrionic. A wild flourish of gestures. Exaggerated manner of speech. Felliniesque music)*

*(In background, inconspicuously holding trays with drinks and appetizers are—*RON *and* DON*—two government officials dressed up as waiters.)*

MAN: *(To audience)* Ladies and Gentlemen: Please. Don't be afraid. Come in. Sit down. Relax. If I eavesdrop on your thoughts, expose your well-guarded secrets it is only because you allow me to do so. You *want* me to do so. Like tuning into your favorite radio station I'll uncover the true frequency of your mind. Open a door to what you thought was forever closed. Shhh...I can feel it coming on now. Shhh! Can you feel it. Yes. *(Offstage, addressing someone in lighting booth)* Could we please bring the lights down on this festive occasion.

(House lights dim)

MAN: Thank you. Much better. Much. No doubt there are things that you are trying to hide from me in this darkness. But I can see them. *Hear* them. Your thoughts transparent like a window to my voice. A lost echo ahead of its source. Shhh. *(Pointing at audience member)* First row. Lady with the Prada purse. There's a cell phone in your purse. On it an important message urgently blinks. Something you need to hear in privacy, *without* your husband listening by your side. Am I right? Please sit down. And don't forget to turn off

your phone. *(He continues to circulate through audience.)*
We all have secrets. Guard our thoughts as if they were
exclusively ours. *Originated* inside us. But we know
that's not true, is it...? This well-meaning *hubris* we
call *thought.* To think our *own* thoughts. As if we could
ever really *own* them with the language of our words.
Thinking my thought is *this!* Saying *this* is my thought...
my desire. *(Isolating another audience member)* Quick!!
Man with beard. Fourth row from back. *You!* Yes you.
Right now you are thinking about the babysitter you
left with the kids so you could come here tonight...
thinking Nadia— (Is that her name?) —thinking Nadia
might have a soft spot for you the way she always stays
late after you already pay her. Ah, if only it could be
you she were putting to bed instead of those little brats?
But no, you must be a gentleman and walk her to the
car. *(Back to audience)* Ladies and Gentlemen! Tonight
I will air out the mystery of your heart and set you free
from the secrets that possess and chain you in their web
of shame. Why...? *Because you want me to.* In the guise of
tonight's entertainment you'll grow less inhibited and
confess all your irresistible secrets to me... *(He now looks
towards a designated spot in the balcony—if theater has
one—and in a more deliberate manner begins addressing the
unseen presidential couple.)* And now...Mister and Mrs
President. *(He bows.)* Our esteemed host and hostess
for this evening's party—if I may train my awesome
powers on you for a brief and cherished moment, I will
unwrap your most private thoughts like the cleverly
wrapped birthday presents you are about to open oh
beloved Mister President. *(Beat)* But wait! *Wait!* An
urgent mental communiqué has just been intercepted...
(More focused, ominous) Beware, Mister President, beware.
The end is terrible. All there at the beginning. The
beginning a foregone conclusion to the end. A public
secret we're all aware of but trying to forget. Children
starved for the sins of their parents. Parents punished

by the orphans they create. Worldwide suffering, hunger...the globalization of pain in a new economy of shame. Will this be your legacy, Mister President? Will this be your legacy?! But wait! Wait! What's this I see? There is more. So much more! *Beware, Mister President, beware.* No...no! No!!!

(Spent and unsteady MAN collapses, as if in a trance. A huge explosion rocks the house. Lights flicker and go abruptly out.)

Scene 2

(Lights back up. Onstage a room in wild disarray)

(Sitting in the middle is the MAN [mindreader] from the previous scene, turban by his feet, head bowed.)

(The two waiters—RON and DON—have shed their waiter uniforms—now wearing patriotic socks, ties, and American flag pins. They are all business. MAN is unconscious.)

RON: *(Reading aloud from transcript)* Beware, Mister President, beware. The end is terrible...*blah blah blah.* The globalization of pain...*blah blah blah*...in a new economy of shame... *blah blah blah. (Stops reading, looks up)* What does it mean? *(Shouts at MAN)* What the fuck does it all mean?!

DON: He can't hear you.

RON: Why not?

DON: Just look at him.

RON: Should we call a doctor?

DON: He'll come around.

RON: *(With violence)* I bet I can wake him.

DON: Wait! *(There's some kind of noise or shift in light.)* President's giving his speech.

(DON *turns on radio and tunes it. Issuing from it is the* PRESIDENT's *voice.)*

(Every time the President comes on the radio, it has shifted to a different location onstage.)

RADIO: Dear fellow Americans...

(They stand and salute. Propping MAN *up between them, still unconscious.)*

RON & DON: God Bless the President!

(As they give a salute, MAN *drops to floor.)*

RADIO—PRESIDENT: Today I ask you to join me from a safe but undisclosed location to inaugurate the titanic struggle against the terror that wants to blind us with fear.

RON: Hey, Don!

(DON ignores him. PRESIDENT continues on radio.)

RADIO—PRESIDENT: Recently I myself have fallen prey to this paralyzing infection of terror.... But with cunning intelligence and a good dose of God's luck, I've been able to narrowly dodge the daily assaults on my personal freedom...and yes, even life.

RON: *(Louder)* Psst! Don!

DON: What Ron? What?

RON: Your pin.

DON: Yeah?

RON: The flag.

DON: What about it?

RON: On your pin.

DON: I'm trying to listen to our President, Ron.

RON: It's upside down.

(DON *looks, sees that* RON *is right. Embarrassed, he quickly flips his flag pin around.*)

DON: Thanks, Ron. Thanks.

(RON *smiles, turns up radio.*)

(*Lights fade...as* PRESIDENT *continues his speech.*)

Scene 3

(MAN *in chair. As before.* RON *and* DON *are nowhere in sight.*)

(WOMAN *enters. She casts a handkerchief across* MAN's *bowed head, as if performing some kind of magic trick. Utters gravely*)

WOMAN: Abracadabra!

(WOMAN *then removes handkerchief and kisses* MAN. *Dazed and disoriented, he lifts his head and opens his eyes just in time to catch her leave.*)

(*Blackout*)

Scene 4

(*Lights back up.* MAN *is conscious. But still disoriented.* RON *and* DON *at his side*)

MAN: What day is it?

RON: What day do you want it to be?

MAN: Where am I?

RON: Where do you think?

MAN: Who are you?

RON: Who wants to know?

MAN: Where am I?

DON: Where do you think?

MAN: *Who are you?*

DON: Who wants to know.

MAN: *Who are you?*

(Briefly strike the pose of waiters, trays up in air.)

RON: *Who do we look like?*

MAN: *Who are you?*

DON: *Who do we look like?*

MAN: *What is this?*

DON: What?

MAN: *What do you want from me?*

DON: You tell us. We're asking the questions. Not you. You tell us what *we* want. Understand?

Scene 5

(WOMAN returns and undresses in half-light, gagging MAN with her belt. Then fiddles with radio. Lee Greenwood singing: God Bless the U S A. *Half-dressed, she commences to lap dance for MAN.)*

WOMAN: Now doesn't that make you feel patriotic?

MAN: I...

WOMAN: *(Grinding his crotch)* Don't lie. I can feel you coming to attention.

(Suddenly—WOMAN hears a noise offstage. She quickly turns off music, then dresses hurriedly and collects her things. Putting an admonishing finger to MAN's lips.)

WOMAN: Shhh!

(Then she exits—just as RON *and* DON *enter pushing a coffee tray. They adjust lights to full. Strangely look around...surveying the room.)*

DON: You feel it *Ron?*

RON: Oh I feel it *Don.* I feel it.

*(*DON *circles* MAN, *sniffing.)*

DON: You smell it Ron?

RON: Mmmm... I smell it Don. I smell it.

DON: Someone has a secret, Ron.

RON: They sure do, Don. They sure do.

*(*DON *pours some coffee.)*

DON: Strong.

RON: Rich.

DON: *(Stirring in milk)* Like a freshly brewed pot of coffee trying to wake someone up. God, I love the aromatic smell of coffee in the morning. Especially when it's raining outside and there's nothing to do indoors. Brazilian, Ethiopian, Sudanese—preferably some *third world* brand if I'm to have my choice.

RON: Who wouldn't. Who wouldn't.

DON: Maybe our guest is thirsty. Ask our guest if he's thirsty?

RON: Would you care for some coffee?

*(*RON *offers* MAN *some coffee, but* DON *quickly intercepts it.)*

DON: Some people, though, prefer it at night you know.

RON: *(Incredulous)* Coffee...?

DON: *(Sipping coffee)* After dinner, with dessert.

RON: No! I find that hard to believe.

DON: Oh yes, Ron. Some people prefer to stay up *all* night, shrouding their little secrets in isolating darkness, refusing to share them with others.

RON: That's not good, Don.

DON: No, Ron, it's not. Secrets are *bad*.

RON: Dark and selfish.

DON: Meant to exclude others. And privilege the few. *(Beat)* You have any secrets Ron?

RON: Not from you Don. *Never* from you.

DON: Good. Cause this certainly isn't the time or place to harbor any secrets.

RON: No it isn't.

DON: Not from me.

RON: No.

DON: *(To* MAN*)* Or us.

RON: *(To* MAN*)* Certainly not from us.

DON: *(Pouring hims coffee)* It's no accident that you're here Achmed, spending this *quality* time with us.

RON: No...no accident at all.

MAN: *(Puzzled)* Achmed...?

DON: Do you believe in accidents Achmed?

(RON *knocks over coffee, splashing* MAN. *He screams.)*

MAN: That's not my name.

DON: How about *Amir*? Is that better?

MAN: *(With emphasis) Amal.* My name is Amal. Means pure.

DON: *(Overlap)* Whatever. I asked if you believe in luck? Or is everything simply the inscrutable will of Allah the Great, Allah the Magnificent?

MAN: *Allah...?*

RON: Is that your name?

MAN: Amal. I told you.

DON: But Amal doesn't have the right ring to it.

RON: Or smell.

DON: Not like Achmed. Or Abdul.

RON: Fee Fie Fo Fum
I smell the thoughts
of a Musilm.

MAN: But I'm not Muslim. I keep telling you. My name
is Amal. Means pure. My parents are from a village
near Calcutta.

RON: Wasn't Ghandi a Muslim?

DON: Hindu I believe.

RON: Are you sure?

DON: Hindus don't eat cows.

RON: What about pigs?

DON: *That's* Muslim. *(Aside)* Not that there's anything
wrong with being Muslim. The Muslim people are an
integral part of our community.

RON: *(Overlap)* Great man, Ghandi. Great man. What
you'd call a real *fuckin* pacifist.

DON: I was in India once. Did you know that? Reading
Salaman Rushdie by the banks of the Ganges.
Picnicking by the Taj Mahal. But then you go into
Calcutta, and there are so many people, so many faces,
you forget who you are. *(Beat)* But we're losing sight
of the real reason we're here. Together. You see, what
concerns us even more than rogue states are *rogue states
of mind*. Whether you come from India or the Arab

Emirates is irrelevant. What we need is your help.
So we can help you.

MAN: What did I do?

RON: That's why you must help us.

DON: So we can help you.

MAN: I don't even know what I did.

DON: It's more what you said, really.

RON: *(Reading transcript)* Beware, Mister President,
beware!

DON: Were those your words?

MAN: I don't remember.

RON: Were you trying to threaten the president...?

DON: Or just warn him?

MAN: I passed out.

RON: And the explosion? What about the fuckin
explosion?

MAN: Must've happened after I collapsed.

DON: Yet somehow, some way, you still managed to
take an un-authorized tour of the President's mind.
Play hide and seek with his expansive thoughts.

MAN: I have no recollection of this whatsoever.

RON: Are you calling the President a liar?

MAN: Of course not. No. But whenever I perform I go
into a kind of... trance.

DON: He felt you doing this, you know. Like some
invisible hand tickling his mind, he felt you reading...

RON: *(Correcting DON/overlap) Stealing...*

DON: ...his most intimate thoughts.

MAN: I never stole anything.

RON: *(Overlap)* Security codes, classified itineraries, covert operations, secret global strategies...

MAN: Does he even know I'm here?

RON: Who? The President?

MAN: Shouldn't someone tell him I'm here?

DON: Didn't I just say...*that*?

RON: Yeah... Didn't he just say that?

DON: *(Laughing)* You think the President doesn't know what's going on here? These are his orders we're carrying out. The President instructed us quite explicitly. He said, in no uncertain terms, he said: Ron, Don...I want you two trustworthy men to go in there and do the *Will of God*. You hear that...? The "Will of God". *(Beat)* You do believe in God, don't you?

MAN: I want to call my lawyer.

DON: First tell us about the dark presentiments you saw lurking on the luminous edge of our beloved President's horizon...

MAN: I'm sorry, but I can't remember a thing. I told you.

DON: *(Overlapping)* We can always help you remember if that's what you'd like? Would you like that? Would you like us to help you?

MAN: This is ridiculous.

DON: Last night...

RON: The party...

DON: The president.

RON: The President.

RON/DON: *(Saluting) The President!*

RON: Tell us about the President's party.

DON: Was the First Lady drunk?

RON: Did they serve those little pigs in a blanket?

DON: Sing raucous patriotic songs?

RON: I love those little pigs in a blanket.

DON: We want to hear everything imaginable.

RON: In the smallest detail possible.

DON: But first we want you to guess who's older.

MAN: Who is older...?

DON: Come on. Give us a live demonstration of your mental *prowess,* your so-called *telepathic* powers. Show us why our esteemed President solicited your services in the first place...

RON: *(Darkly)* ...and why he regretted doing so right after.

MAN: Regretted? But the President is my biggest fan. I—

RON: Tell that to your agent.

MAN: My agent?

DON: If he'll return your call.

RON: *Beware Mister President, beware!*

MAN: That was all just part of my act. You know that.

RON: Your act...?

MAN: That's right. It was a show. That's all. A lousy piece of theater.

DON: The theater has always been a very dangerous place. We cannot forget that. Look at Abraham Lincoln.

(RON *makes a gun with his fingers, points it at* MAN's *head.)*

RON: *Boom!*

(Beat)

DON: So...what's the answer?

MAN: Answer?

DON: Who's older? Ron...

RON: ...or Don? *(Beat)* Go ahead and guess. You only lose one digit on each hand for each wrong answer. Kidding. Only kidding. But you better guess right.

MAN: Are you asking me to *perform* on command?

RON: What's wrong with that? You are a magician, no?

MAN: A mind reader actually...

DON: Terrorist, magician. Not much difference really. The way you blow things up. Make them disappear. Except that the magician usually restores them to their previous state. But not you. No, not you. *(Beat)* Know what lies at the opposite end of terrorism...? *Tourism.* Tourism in a practical sense—*art* in a more theoretical one.

MAN: But I'm not a real magician. Let alone terrorist. I told you, I'm—

DON: Shhh!! Do I look like I'm done? I'll let you know when I'm done. *(Pause)* Now whereas art tries to bring forth light through meaning; terrorism appropriates meaning and creates darkness. This is most evident in the hastiness of its destruction. The potent but core simplicity with which a *single* match can bring down the entire forest. It's always easier to destroy something than to build it. Don't you agree?

MAN: Absolutely, I agree absolutely but...you've got the wrong man here.

DON: *(Overlapping, as if reading a slogan)*
TERRORISM THEREFORE IS THE ANTITHESIS OF ART.

MAN: You're talking to the wrong person.

DON: We'll see about that.

MAN: I'm not who you think I am.

RON: Then who are you?

MAN: I want my lawyer now!

DON: I'll be your lawyer.

RON: I thought I was.

DON: We can take turns. First you...

RON: Then me.

DON: Two for the price of one.

RON: I object.

DON: I sustain.

(They laugh.)

DON: Ron, hand me that worn out document in the bottom drawer.

RON: You mean the United States Constitution, Don?

DON: Yeah, that old thing. *(He unfurls the parchment.)* Want to see magic? Watch this. *(Beat)* Ron, hand me a marker.

(RON hands him one. DON ostentatiously crosses something out.)

DON: That was the Fifth amendment. Want to see some more magic? Clause Fourteen—Search and Seizure. Gone. First Amendment—Freedom of Speech. Gone. Hell, let's expedite matters and get rid of the whole thing, what do you say?

(More laughter as they rip it up like confetti. MAN stands, resolute.)

MAN: I'd like to go now. Can I go now? When can I leave?

DON: Go...? You don't want to go. Where would you go? In your pajamas, without your shoes?

RON: Just let the thankless fuck go.

DON: Out there the streets are crying for fresh sacrifice. The gutters thirsty for blood. We brought you here for your own good. Out of consideration for your own safety.

RON: *(Motioning to door)* Go ahead and go. Walk out that door and see how far you get in those award winning pajamas.

DON: After all, we're here to perform *humanitarian intervention.* You want to go back outside, be our guest...leave. But don't be surprised if the door locks behind you.

RON: Your assets all frozen.

(MAN takes a step but...hesitates.)

(WOMAN walks out onstage in her new dress as if its a fashion runway, again unnoticed.)

DON: *(Picks up old dress)* Wife missing and unaccounted for.

MAN: Wife?

DON: *(Regarding the empty dress)* Don't you love your wife?

MAN: I'm not married.

DON: The report shows you live with a woman. A female who shares your last name.

MAN: *(Low)* You mean my sister.

DON: Is that what we mean? I'm not so sure. How about you? How sure are you?

MAN: Is she here? My sister...?

DON: Stick around, find out.

MAN: Just tell me is she alright? Is she alright?

RON: Or you can go. It's entirely up to you. Entirely up to you.

(Lights out)

Scene 6

(MAN alone on stage—all tied up, trying to wiggle himself free.)

(Radio offers another presidential speech from yet another location on stage.)

RADIO—PRESIDENT: Dear fellow Americans, Due to the continued threat to my well being, I am speaking to you from a new undisclosed location to assure you that our issued warnings are not idle or exaggerated security alerts but *real* threats to the American way of life and the freedom we take for granted.

(MAN manages to free one hand. Applause from radio.)

RADIO—PRESIDENT: Like concerned parents, we in government are constantly asking what we can do to protect you, our children?

(More applause. MAN frees other hand.)

RADIO—PRESIDENT: And like it or not—you are all my children even though most of you didn't vote for me. Why, just the other morning I met a farmer working his field, and I said to him, Mister Farmer, I said, plant your crops for tomorrow will be a bountiful harvest. And we had an understanding between us that went deeper than any words. More akin to the magic of prayer.

(MAN *frees his legs, stands, stretches. Ropes slack at his feet*)

(MAN *goes to door. Thinks. Then returns calmly to chair,
sits down and waits*)

(*Lights out*)

Scene 7

(*School bell rings.* WOMAN *is sitting in* MAN'*s chair,
talking to* RON *and* DON. MAN *is absent from room.
Overlap with radio speech above.*)

WOMAN: As you might know I once worked directly for
the President. Shared his most *intimate* thoughts. On an
almost daily basis.

DON: We didn't know that.

WOMAN: How could you?

RON: Cool.

WOMAN: I was a stewardess on Air Force One. Still
have the uniform at home to prove it. Such loud
striking colors. Sometimes, late at night or in the small
hours of the morning, I find myself sitting there in my
nightgown staring at this uniform, the way it hangs
there in the breeze of my closet, dangling like I was
still inside it. Other times, when I get sad and lonely,
I'll actually put it on...I'll close my eyes and slip on the
uniform, then turn on the vacuum cleaner so that its
loud roar will help me imagine myself back on that
presidential plane. With the President at my side.
More pretzels Mister President? Be careful when you chew.
I tell you, those days will always have a special place
in my heart. Serving the President his little snacks and
coffee, sharing the endless open sky with him where
all the great decisions of mankind were made. And no
matter how much turbulence we hit, this man I tell you,

never once spilled a drop of coffee. A steady man for unsteady times. Although I do remember this one scary time when the plane began to nose-dive. And he came right up to me—as close as I am to both of you now—and he said: Here, young lady, he said, take it. I am handing you my parachute because I am just the President, but you, you after all are a potential mother for our country. *(Suddenly bitter)* Later that day I found out it was just a drill, a stupid *emergency* drill. But I'd still like to think that he'd have given me his parachute if the plane were really about to crash. That's the kind of man he is. The kind of smile he had.

RON: Then why did you leave...?

WOMAN: Why did I...

RON: Yeah, if you liked the job so much, why did they fire you?

DON: Ron!

WOMAN: That's okay.

RON: *(To DON)* What? You really think they gave her a paid vacation.

WOMAN: One day, thirty thousand feet above everything, in the middle of nowhere, the President asks for his coffee. So I pour it for him in his sterilized presidential cup. But I'm still using cream instead of milk. How was I to know he was on a diet. No one told me. I don't *read* minds. All I know is that once he tasted his coffee, he isn't smiling anymore.

RON: And they canned your ass for that?

DON: That's not fair.

WOMAN: But I don't blame him. After all this is our *President*. There can be no margin for error as far as the President is concerned.

RON: Harsh.

WOMAN: Which is why I can't stress enough the importance of what goes on here. The *responsibility* bestowed upon the two of you...Ron, Don.

DON: Acutally he's Ron

RON: ...he's Don.

WOMAN: ...to make sure the President's thoughts are in safe custody. *(Beat)* But if this...*man*, this so-called *mindreader*, has really had the opportunity to read the President's mind, then all is in jeopardy. Because once you've learned to read, you'll no doubt want to write. And no man should undertake it upon himself to interpret, or worse yet *counterfeit*, the President's thoughts. *(Beat)* Speaking of which...where is our telepathic guest anyway?

RON: They're giving him the house tour.

WOMAN: House tour?

DON: They're acquainting him with all the various *linguistic* instruments at our disposal.

WOMAN: Good, very good. I'm all for a little persuasion.

DON: Not that we'd ever dream of using these so-called resources

RON: No, never.

DON: *(Overlapping)* But I think just *seeing* them might do him a world of good. Help open up new avenues of thought. The shiny penetrating Black Slave. The handheld incandescent torch. Gold plated pliers... they're showing him all the different kinds of tools confiscated from all those backwards countries that have helped stubborn people like him communicate more freely throughout the ages.

WOMAN: For your sake, let's hope that he outgrows his shyness. Because it's only fair that I give you a heads up here. Let you know that things are in *flux*. The

department—*along with the rest of our world in fact*—
is being restructured.

RON: Restructured...?

WOMAN: There are only two rules in life. First Rule is:
There is always a victim. Second rule is: *Don't ever* be
the victim. You can ignore the first rule, but God help
you, don't ever forget the second.

(School bell rings.)

DON: We won't forget.

RON: You can count on us.

WOMAN: Good. Because this isn't some game we're
playing. *(Crossing to window. The distant sound of
explosions, rumbling.)* Every day more buildings are
destroyed. Monuments leveled. Our open society is
quickly closing. And like expert...*mindreaders* we must
now be preemptive to keep death at arms length and
make terrorism childproof again.

RON: We won't disappoint you.

WOMAN: Just get him to talk.

DON: We'll find out what you need.

WOMAN: I'll be watching you. And just like I'm
watching you, there's always someone watching me.
There are video feeds all around us. All the way up to
the President himself...and then...to God. But by that
point, what would be the difference I ask you, what?

Scene 8

(DON *meditates.* RON *is pacing.* DON *meditates, beads in hand. Still no sign of* MAN.*)*

RON: What time is it?

DON: Relax will you.

RON: I thought he was supposed to back by now.

DON: He'll be back.

RON: When?

DON: You remind me of this lunatic cab driver I once had to the airport. Drove like a maniac the whole time—slamming the accelerator, the brakes, the accelerator—cursing every time someone cut him off, shouting: *(With accent) I can not control them. I can not control them! (Beat)* You should do what I do.

RON: Oh yeah?

DON: Take a deep breath and close your eyes.

(RON *tries to meditate. Stops)*

RON: I can't. You heard her.... They're restructuring. *Restructuring!*

DON: Avoid the negative, focus on the positive. That's what I do.

RON: She got some nerve coming in here, talking that kind of shit. Restructure this...reorganize that... Fuck her!

DON: Here. *(Proudly exhibiting a photo from his wallet)* Ever see this...? That's my boy...Henry.

RON: *(Inspecting photo)* Oh yeah...good looking kid. *(Holds up photo to* DON'*s face.)* I can see the resemblance.

DON: Thanks.

RON: But the real question is, how does he sleep at night?

DON: *(Disgusted)* Don't even ask.

RON: That's the real question.

DON: *(Overriding) Water!* He shouts in the middle of the night. *I need water!* And I'll say, *Shhhh! Momma is asleep.* But he doesn't care. What the fuck does he care— *the little terrorist—blackmailing me with my wife's fragile sleep—water, water!!* But I love him, the little rascal. I really do.

RON: Man, it's a good thing I don't have children, because just hearing that story makes my blood boil.

DON: That's why I meditate. Here. Maybe this'll help. *(He hands RON meditation beads.)* Just don't shove 'em up your ass.

RON: Very funny.

(RON tries to again. DON joins him, offering example.)

DON: Focus on your breathing. Empty your mind. Make everything one. Make everything connected. All the Good, the Evil. You, me, him. Her!

RON: *(Off "her")* Fuck her! *(Suddenly afraid)* Think she's watching us now?

DON: What?

RON: You think she's watching us!??

DON: I don't know.

RON: Is she there? She's there, isn't she. She's there now.

DON: Do you want her to be there? Do you *need* her to be there?

RON: *(Lowering voice)* No but sometimes I feel like I need watching, Don. I need watching! *(He suddenly kicks over* MAN's *chair.)* Where the fuck is he anyway?!

DON: Breathe in, breathe out...

(Again RON *tries to meditate. Can't)*

(Then a thud as MAN *is thrown into room. A heap on the floor.)*

(Blackout)

Scene 9

*(*RON *is furiously typing away as* MAN *talks. Taking his confession.* DON *drinking coffee)*

MAN: My first magic show was a complete disaster.

RON: Now we're getting somewhere. Finally!!!

MAN: I couldn't have been more than seven or eight at the time—and I remember digging my hand deep into my magician's hat for the rabbit—

RON: *(Correcting a typo)* Slower!

MAN: —but when I pulled out the rabbit it was dead!! Poisoned.

DON: Was this your first encounter with terrorism?

MAN: Terrorism...?

DON: What else would you call it?

MAN: I don't know... But after that day I suffered stage fright for many years.

RON: Stage fright is a form of terrorism too, you know....

MAN: Are we almost done?

RON: Almost. Almost. Oh... She's gonna love this. Love it!

DON: Why do you think someone would do such a thing? Poison a poor defenseless bunny?

MAN: I don't know.

DON: Not even after all these years?

MAN: No.

RON: I find that hard to believe.

MAN: I never did anything to hurt anyone.

DON: You must've pissed someone off. I mean for them to do such a thing. There'd have to be a reason.

RON: (*Overlap, stops typing*) What did you do? Just tell us what the *fuck* you did!

MAN: Nothing. I did nothing.

DON: But you were tormented.

MAN: Yes.

DON: For *nothing*...?

MAN: I guess so...yes.

DON: Let me share a little secret with you for a change. Nothing's for Nothing. *Not even nothing.*

RON: (*With a flourish*) Ta da! Done! (*Yanks sheet out of type writer*) Should I read it back to him.

DON: What for. Just get his signature.

(*They hand* MAN *the "confession" he reads it in disgust, disbelief.*)

MAN: I can't sign this.

DON: Sure you can.

MAN: This isn't what I said.

RON: (*Laugh*) It's what we heard.

DON: *Sign!*

MAN: *(To* DON*)* Have you *read* this nonsense?

DON: We just *wrote* it, didn't we? Didn't we?

RON: *(Overlapping)* What you call *poetic license.*

DON: *(Conspiratorial to* MAN*)* Ron, I'll have you know helped draft the Domestic Security Enhancement Act. Isn't that right Ron?

RON: *(False modesty)* Just the part about terrorism, Don.

MAN: But this...this is all your lies...*your* inventions.

RON: *(Under his breath)* There he goes again.

DON: Yes. And over the years we've discovered quite a few truths with our falsehoods, haven't we Ron?

RON: Without a doubt Don.

DON: Who knows, *Faquhar,* by the time we're through with our lies we might even find out that you're innocent.

MAN: I'm not Faquhar.

RON: Then maybe you're also *not* innocent. Just because you're willing to die for something doesn't make it right.

MAN: My name is Amal. Means pure. You already know that. You—

DON: I've had enough of his shit.

(They gag MAN.*)*

DON: Do us a favor. Just read the damn thing and sign it. Or you can just sign and not read. Whatever you want—just do it. Like your sister.

RON: For your sister!

DON: And please—use your real name for once. We're all running out of time. Especially you.

RON: You heard the man.

(Abruptly RON *smacks* MAN *across face.)*

DON: What did you do that for?

RON: *(Shrugs)* Ask him, he's the mind reader.

(They exit, laughing.)

(Lights iris on MAN. RON *and* DON *vanish in darkness.)*

(With a great effort we hear the MAN*'s voice, as if
telepathically escaping his head, mouth still gagged.)*

MAN: *(Voice)* Run, my sister, run. If indeed I have the
power of telepathy as they seem to think I do, heed
my warning, sister, and run. Don't ever stop running.
Because the only comfort I have is to know that you
are far away from here...my sister. This morning, when
I was shaving, I saw a bug crawling on the mirror.
At first I was about to squash it, but then I started
wondering if it could see itself in the glass, poor little
thing. It looked so lost and confused I couldn't really
kill it.

Scene 10

(Lights up to reveal MAN *hanging from ceiling, passed out,
swinging slightly back and forth. Tape across his mouth)*

*(*DON *meditates serenely in front. An occasional contented
hum escapes his lips. A beat)*

*(*WOMAN *enters, watches* DON *meditate. Gives* MAN
another shove—he swings higher, almost keeping time.)

WOMAN: Are you praying?

DON: God forbid.

WOMAN: I thought you were praying. Walking in like
that. Seeing you on the ground. I thought—

DON: *(Overlap)* I'm learning to listen to the silence. Greatest trick of all, you know, is the trick of silence.

WOMAN: Maybe you can teach it to me some day. I'm looking to enrich my repertoire, you know.

DON: O K. Which is worse: the cries borne out of silence—or the silence that follows our cries?

WOMAN: Is that a trick question?... *(She approaches* MAN, *who is hung from ceiling.)* Or why you've got him all hung up?

DON: *(Shrugs)* When was the last time you prayed?

WOMAN: Why would I pray? ...I'm not the victim.

DON: *(Beat)* Guess how many times we breathe in a day. On average. In one day. Go ahead, guess.

WOMAN: In and out. Or just in?

DON: Both.

WOMAN: I don't know. Ten thousand?

DON: Thirty-eight-thousand-three-hundred-eighty-three breaths in one day. Once I spend a whole week just counting my breaths, doing nothing else. *(He breathes deeply.)* Talk about a humbling narcissistic experience. Each breath like a present. A gift. An internal ocean waxing and waning to the tide of my soul. *(Breathes)* Peace through inner wisdom. That's what I say. Let go of your desires and you let go of your suffering. But lately I've discovered I have no desires to let go of. Only fear.

WOMAN: Poor Ron. Must be hard being you.

DON: I'm Don.

WOMAN: Of course. I'm sorry. I should've known. Where is Ron anyway?

DON: Therapy. Says it makes him less violent. But I haven't really seen any difference. *(Beat)* Told him he should meditate.

WOMAN: Like you.

DON: Like me. *(Breathes deeply, meditates briefly)*

WOMAN: I've always been attracted to men who can think. But a man who can think quietly, in silence, that's *really* something, isn't it? *(Beat)* Come here... *(Trying to recall his name)*

DON: *(Completing)* Don.

WOMAN: (Overlapping) Don.

(DON does, WOMAN hikes up her skirt. And places his hand on her sex. In background, MAN starts to shift and moan.)

WOMAN: I want you to teach me the secret of your *complex* silence and what it shrouds from us.

DON: I'm not sure I know what you mean.

WOMAN: As a young impressionable girl I always thought everyone could read my mind same way they could see my panty-line or the nipples poking through my shirt. Now I know better. I think *obliquely.* Arrive indirectly at all my conclusions. As if by sheer... accident. Always surprising myself as if I were... *someone else. Is that me thinking this? Did I really just think that...? What am I really thinking now?* Like every thought was its own little secret.

(WOMAN hastily undoes DON's pants, gropes him to her.)

DON: Are you sure you want to do this?

WOMAN: Teach me. Yes, teach me to...*meditate* the way you do. When the unthinkable and unspeakable are one.

DON: What about Ron?

(WOMAN commences fucking.)

WOMAN: *(Self-absorbed)* One thought always spying on another, shrouded by another, so that soon all boundaries are erased between the one who asks the question and the one who gives the answer.

DON: *(Breathless, panting)* I said, What if Ron comes in...?

WOMAN: (Cutting him off) Fuck Ron!! Times like this you have to think of yourself. *For* yourself!

(Full throttle, mindless fucking. The sex ineluctable)

DON: *(Re: MAN)* And him?

(They now turn to take MAN in, he groans louder.)

DON: He's starting to come around.

WOMAN: Good! Now we can see how good he is at keeping real secrets.

(They continue fucking harder and harder in front of MAN.)

(MAN—starts to get an aroused look on his face, as if vicariously enjoying their sex. Reading their minds. After a while, MAN begins to appropriate their climax:)

MAN: *(Enraptured)* I...I'm coming. I'm coming.

WOMAN: Did you say something?

DON: *(Climaxing)* I just came.

WOMAN: *(Disappointed)* That's what I thought. *(She wipes the premature ejaculation from her thigh in disgust.)*

Scene 11

(WOMAN sits half-dressed in chair in front of MAN, who is still hanging by his arms. She seems to be in a state of extreme arousal, approaching orgasm, eyes closed, purring.)

(Both RON and DON are out.)

WOMAN: *(Enraptured)* Oh my God! I can feel you thinking about me. How lightly you touch me with your thoughts. Like sunlight reaching across a million light years of cold dark space to warm my cheek. Think of me. *Memorize* me. Make me yours. Oh God I'm gonna come, Oh God! Oh God! Oh God! Look at me look at me look at me! *(She comes and quickly regains composure)* What the fuck are you looking at?! You scum! *(Again, she closes eyes, begins to approach climax.)* Oh God this is incredible! You're doing it to me again. Oh God! No hands, no objects. Oh yes. My most intimate secret about to be exposed. What can be more *penetrating* than the transmission of pure thought. From my mind directly into yours. To be *mindfucked* like this... by a *mindfucker* like you... Oh God! *(She bites her lip as she comes. Then snaps to attention.)* Shhh! You hear something...? I thought I heard something. *(Listening)* Shh! Is it them? Are they back? Did you hear them? *(She hurriedly gets dressed, begins to untie MAN, lowering him from ceiling.)* Better not to talk, not to think. *(Beat)* Start thinking and right away you're in trouble. I swear, better to be an atheist than to question your own thought. Are you hot? Is it too bright in here? Thirsty? Are you hot? Did I just ask that? *(She helps MAN into chair.)* These are just some of the questions I ask myself every minute of the day. What about yourself? What questions do you ask?

MAN: *Why me?*

WOMAN: What?

MAN: Why am I still here?!

WOMAN: *(Incredulous)* Why are you here?

MAN: That's what I'm asking. Yes. Why are you doing this to me?

WOMAN: Why does everyone always ask that question? Innocent or not doesn't really matter. You are the stone we throw at the world.

MAN: *(Overlap)* But I didn't do anything. You know that.

WOMAN: Don't flatter yourself. We're not just picking on you—*sallem allechem*—we're picking on everyone who *looks* like you. You want we could pick on your sister instead?

MAN: No.

WOMAN: Then let's continue where we left off. *Why do you hate us?*

(WOMAN finishes untying MAN.)

MAN: Hate you...?! I don't...

WOMAN: You heard me!

MAN: *(Overlapping)* No...I...

WOMAN: (Overlap) I can tell. Why do you hate me. What have I ever done to you? What?!

MAN: I don't hate you.

WOMAN: Of course you do. I can smell it from here. Your hatred is profound...zoological. *(She sneezes.)*

MAN: Bless you.

WOMAN: Thanks. *(Beat)* Hiroshima, Nagasaki, El Salvador, the Gulf War... These are not reasons, just excuses. I want to know why you really hate *me*. Why *me* in particular?!

MAN: I don't—

WOMAN: *(Overlapping)* I bet you weren't very popular as a child. Most people who go into magic aren't very popular. They do it to impress their friends. Gain approval. *(She picks up rope from floor hands it to him.)* Tie me up.

MAN: Excuse me?

WOMAN: You heard me. Upside down. Just like you were...before.

(WOMAN makes herself available to be restrained. MAN hesitates, but then complies.)

WOMAN: Must be hard on you. The strain of maintaining all these *uncirculated* secrets...these *lies*... I could never do that. Soon as I start *thinking* about *what* exactly I'm thinking I'm fucked. *(Re: ropes)* Make it tighter! *(Beat)* Maybe that's why I'm so messed up. *(Re: ropes)* I said tighter. *(Beat)* So how does one assign guilt in a universe where the hand is often quicker than the eye—and the word faster than our thought? *(Pause)* No. Better not to talk, to think. Just because we can, doesn't mean we should. And just because we might actually be guilty, doesn't mean we'll let you punish us. *(Re: ropes)* Hurry up already!

MAN: I've never done this before.

WOMAN: Hit me.

MAN: What?

WOMAN: You heard me. Don't look so innocent. I've seen the way you treat your women, how you cover them from head to toe like some shameful secret. Hit me!

MAN: I can't.

WOMAN: Hit me you sack of shit, or I'll have 'em rape your sister.

(MAN *does, gently.*)

WOMAN: *Harder! I untied you for a reason Gunga Din.*

(WOMAN *now hangs from ceiling—like* MAN *was earlier. She swings.*)

WOMAN: Again.

(MAN *hits* WOMAN *harder.*)

WOMAN: Again.

(*Harder*)

WOMAN: Again.

(MAN *lets* WOMAN *have it.*)

MAN: *You like that?!*

WOMAN: (*Perversely*) That's more like it. Now why do you hate us?

MAN: I don't hate—

WOMAN: (*Screaming*) Again! Hit me again. And this time, *Daddy*, you better fuckin mean it!

(MAN *prepares to swing. Black out. As voice of* PRESIDENT *interrupts.*)

Scene 12

(PRESIDENT *interrupts the beating, as* RON *and* DON *rush in to rescue* WOMAN *and slap* MAN *around.*)

(*As the speech goes on, they violently handcuff* MAN *and force him into a narrow upright coffin.*)

RADIO—PRESIDENT: At ease my fellow Americans, at ease. You can hear my voice, but do any of you know where I am...? My disembodied *voice* reaching you from the furthest corner of the earth like a lost dream from which I can't wake up. A dream of wide open spaces.

Where no terrorist can hide and every citizen is safe.
The other night—or should I say day since it's hard
to tell one from the other where I am currently
sequestered—the depopulated world of my dreams
was once more haunted by the recurring image of a girl
running across the sand. Birds—hawking and planing—
pursued her from all corners of the sky. But strange
thing is, as she runs, this girl leaves no footprints in the
sand. As if she was never there...

(A rush of static infiltrates the PRESIDENT'*s speech. Soon we
hear another familiar voice. It is the* MAN'*s voice—stepping
on the* PRESIDENT'*s lines, also issuing from the radio as he's
being violently forced to enter the coffin.)*

RADIO—MAN'S VOICE: Run, sister, run. And do not
stop. Never stop.

RADIO—PRESIDENT: The insurgents, as you can hear,
are trying to obstruct me, my Voice, but being the
Conscience of America I will prevail.

RADIO—MAN'S VOICE: *(Stepping over)* And if you can't
hide in the distance, dear sister, bury yourself in time.
You can only hold your breath for so long. And the
sand is so hot and full of crabs...

*(Explosion heard through radio, as they slam coffin door on
Man.)*

RADIO—PRESIDENT: Like the beating of my heart,
the bombs go off. Our lives forever regulated by some
unseen metronome ticking away the minutes of some
hidden timebomb.

*(Underneath, broken over the airwaves, we simultaneously
hear the voice being squelched.)*

RADIO—MAN'S VOICE: Watch out sister! Watch out!!!

RADIO—PRESIDENT: But in the end...in the end we'll be
better for all this. Stronger. Surveillance will breed a

new kind of confidence... Because as you know—
you only learn to love something once it's gone.
And so we love our country even more now when
she's threatened. *(Beat)* And now if you could all rise
and join me in the Pledge of allegiance...

RON: *(Hitting coffin)* Stand up!

ALL: *(Including radio)* I pledge allegiance to the flag of
the United States of America and to the Republic for
which it stands, one Nation *under God*...indivisible,
with liberty and justice for all.

(Ear against wood, listening to inside of coffin)

RON: He didn't say—Under God.

DON: You sure?

RON: I'm sure.

DON: I thought I heard him.

RON: Uh-uh. That was me.

(Explosion shakes room.)

DON: Fuck! That was close.

RON: *(Crossing to window)* You're not going to believe
this.

DON: What?

RON: That, Don, was the Statue of Liberty.

DON: No!! *(He races to window.)*

RON: I bet he knew all along. He and his sister!

DON: I can't believe this!

RON: I bet they planned it.

DON: I just can't believe it.

*(Another explosion. They duck. Slowly approach coffin with
MAN inside it.)*

DON: What's he smiling at now? What?

MAN: *(From inside coffin)* I'm not smiling.

DON: Like fuck you're not. No one likes to be blown apart. Not even a statue.

RON: He's doing it again.

(They both pull out their guns and aim them at the upright closed coffin, slowly backing away in fear.)

DON: Make him stop. Whatever it is he's doing, I want him to stop!

(Explosion. Lights out)

Scene 13

(RON is cleaning up and sweeping debris from previous explosions. MAN slumped in chair)

(WOMAN enters.)

WOMAN: You still here...?

RON: Someone's got to clean this mess up.

(WOMAN lifts coffin lid, inspects the unconscious MAN with bruises. Shuts it)

WOMAN: You really enjoy this, don't you?

RON: What?

WOMAN: They say that torture is a way to kill someone more than once. The need to purge our anger and violence. But you want to know what I think...? I think that no matter how hard we listen to one another or how *attentive* we become, we can never *really* understand another person in this world—only *dominate* them. Because if you truly *understood* them. Entered inside their heads to align yourself with their thoughts... their *perspective*...then you'd loose your own point of view and become them. And then what...what then?! *(Beat)* But you...you are different from *them* aren't you? You and Ron are as different as day and night.

RON: I *am* Ron.

WOMAN: I meant Don. You are different from Don, Ron.

RON: Different is not always better.

WOMAN: In this case it is. *(Beat)* Almost done?

RON: You can help me if you want.

(WOMAN wipes floor with finger, tastes it.)

WOMAN: Blood...?

RON: I'm supposed to mop up all the red blotches from the floor and furniture.

WOMAN: Is it blood that makes up a family? Or the spilling of blood? What do you think?

RON: Don's the one with the kid.

(WOMAN removes dress over her head, revealing a sexy thong.)

RON: What are you doing?

WOMAN: Helping.

RON: I don't understand.

WOMAN: *(Flaunting her body)* Is it hot in here— or just more bad global warming?

RON: Please put that back on.

WOMAN: Okay, but first touch me.

RON: What?

(WOMAN closes her eyes.)

WOMAN: Touch me anywhere you want. Go on. Just touch me. Are you touching me now?

(RON *does.*)

RON: Yes.

WOMAN: I can't feel it. Touch me somewhere else. Are you touching me now?

RON: Yes.

WOMAN: Why can't I feel you. Why the fuck can't I feel you?! I want you touch me where I can feel it. Touch me in a way so I know I'm still here. With you. At my side. *(She drags him to coffin, lies down)* Because if we're gonna have sex—you and me—it's gotta be now. Right this minute. Because later on I might not want it anymore. Desire is all about urgency. And even as I say this to you now, already part of me is thinking it's over between us. Well...? Is it. Over?

RON: Did I do something wrong?

WOMAN: What kind of a question is that? We've all done something wrong. Something we can't see. Won't admit. You, me, everyone.

RON: I don't want to punish you. *(Kicking coffin)* Like him.

WOMAN: That's what you say now. But how can I trust you when I don't even trust myself.

RON: You must be a very lonely person then.

WOMAN: Not as lonely as you. You with your dirty little secret.

RON: Secret? What secret is that?

(WOMAN *crosses to* MAN *who is still unconscious.*)

WOMAN: Maybe I should ask him.

(WOMAN *begins to open coffin.* RON *slams it shut.*)

RON: *(Threatened)* I don't have any secrets.

WOMAN: *(Re: MAN)* I bet he'll know.

RON: Just put your dress back on.

WOMAN: Are you telling me what to do?

RON: Please.

WOMAN: Don't you like the way I look? Most men can't get enough.

RON: Don will be back any minute.

WOMAN: *(Harsh whisper)* For your information, Don was a *big* disappointment in that arena. *(Beat)* But don't think I don't know what's going on here. *Because I know.* I know everything about you. And my advice to you is: Keep your guard up. Maintain your vigil. Don't ever be the victim.

RON: I am not the victim. *He* is!

WOMAN: Is that what *Don* keeps telling you?

RON: *(Angry, overlap)* Keep him out of it!

WOMAN: Fine. Fine. But I know better.

RON: I have nothing to hide. Nothing.

WOMAN: Of course not. Of course not. Coffee?

RON: No thanks.

WOMAN: Suit yourself. *(Insinuating)* But I could use something *hot* to warm me up right now. And I know it's not going to be you. *(She kisses his lips and whispers harshly:) Virgin!*

(WOMAN then stalks out. Disgusted, RON wipes away her kiss.)

RON: Cunt!

(Banging on coffin. MAN inside)

RON: Wake *up*!! Wake up! I thought we made it clear to you. No more sleeping. Passing out is one thing, but

sleeping is another. *(Mulling over, bitter)* Virgin!! Me...?
I'm not a faggot. Who said faggot?! *(To* MAN*)* Up up
up! I'm tired of being alone here with you. Time to live
in the world you've helped destroy. Open your eyes...
faggot! *(More mulling)* Fuck her I'm a virgin. *(To* MAN*)*
Wake up and keep me company but not another
fucking *word*. I'm tired of having you undress my
thoughts in that nudist colony you call your mind.
(Self-consumed) I might've been a virgin once, but who
wasn't. *(To* MAN*)* Hey, even as a twelve year-old virgin
I could still suck my own dick. Now of course I no
longer have that skill or flexibility, let alone the
acrobatic curiosity to do so. But does that make me gay?
I don't think so. But it is something I wanted to share
with you and only you. This secret. Something I never
told anyone before but thought we might be able to talk
about. My genius for auto-fellatio. What do you think?
Am I right? What do you think?

*(*DON *pops up from behind some furniture.)*

DON: Disgusting, Ron! That's what I think! Disgusting!!

RON: Jesus, Don! What are you dong here?

DON: *(Laughs)* Sucking my own dick.

RON: But I thought you were—

DON: Out?

RON: *(Embarrassed, back pedaling)* Hey... you know what
I just said...about sucking my *you-know-what*...I just said
that to test him. See if he was awake. Shit wasn't really
for real you know.

DON: Oh, yeah. *(Makes slurping noises)*

RON: Cut it out, Don.

(More slurping noises.)

RON: Stop it!

DON: Like a fuckin dog, Ron, a dog.

RON: It's not true.

DON: Whatever.

(DON *slurps more.*)

(RON *turns viciously on* MAN, *flings open coffin lid.*)

RON: *(Yanks him out)* What the fuck are you smiling at?

MAN: I'm not smiling—

RON: *(Overlapping)* Sitting there in your terrorist pajamas, given to you by your terrorist sister, thinking terrorist thoughts, giving off your terrorist smell, with that terrorist smile. That fuckin smile!! You don't need the mark of Cain across your forehead to let us know who you are, cause by the time we're through here I'm gonna fuck the terrorist shit right out of you.

(RON *bends* MAN *over chair and prepares to rape him.*)

DON: Whoah, Ron! Relax.

RON: And when I'm done fucking you with my dick, I'm gonna sodomize you with Don's dick over there.

DON: Ron!

RON: What?

DON: You're getting way too invested here.

RON: You're right. I'm sorry.

DON: Way too invested. Lowering yourself to his level like that.

RON: I apologize for my indelicate outburst. It's just that these people and their middle-eastern *reticence*... you know how it gets me.

DON: I know. I know. But anger never solved anything. Think like the naked Archimedes in his bath, think rationally, with patience. Luxuriously.

RON: *(To* MAN, *incensed)* You smile and flirt with us like some coy *virgin.* Ignoring our questions and resisting our advances. But not for long. We can make you feel loved. Wanna feel loved?

DON: I'm not sure you want to go there, Ron.

RON: No, I don't. But someone's gotta do the dirty work around here. And unfortunately it's always me. Never you, Don, never *you! (Removes belt, resumes rape position)* Bend over, mind-fucker!

MAN: No. Please...

DON: Think of therapy. Count to ten.

RON: *(To* DON*)* What? You think I enjoy this? I don't enjoy this. You just happen to be catching me in an *engorged* patriotic mood.

MAN: Please... Don't...

*(*RON *ignores* MAN, *prepares to rape him.)*

RON: I'm doing this for my country. *My* country. I'm not the victim. He is. *(To* MAN*)* Say it. *"I am the victim." Say it!*

MAN: I am the victim.

RON: Louder!

MAN: I am the victim.

RON: Repeat after me.

DON: Christ! I'm gonna get some coffee.

RON/MAN *(Together)* I am the victim.

DON: Anyone want some coffee?

*(*MAN *raped in background. Suddenly calls for* DON*)*

MAN: Don! Don!

*(*DON *returns.)*

DON: What now Ron?

RON: *(Still vigorously raping)* I didn't call your name.

MAN: I did.

DON: You...?

MAN: But it's what *he's* thinking the whole time he's doing me, thinking about you.

RON: That's a lie!

MAN: *(Falsetto)* Don! Don!

RON: You fuckin cocksucker.

MAN: Look who's talking.

RON: I'll show you. *(Begins to rape MAN more violently)* I'll show you!!

DON: *(exiting)* I'm getting coffee. If you change your minds, let me know.

(Lights out)

Scene 14

(MAN in chair. WOMAN enters with a fresh plate of food for him. Sets it down, waits. MAN looks away.)

WOMAN: You mind...? *(She picks at his food.)* They tell me you haven't eaten in almost a week. I can understand that...after what you've been through. But don't you think you're over-reacting just a little bit.

MAN: They...they...

WOMAN: What precisely are you trying to do here? With that kind of behavior? You think having a secret really makes you more interesting?

MAN: They...they....

WOMAN: So they had a little fun with you. Maybe they should've been more tender. Loving. So what? I was raped too you know, at the tender age of twelve, then impressed into the sex industry in the Bangkok Patpang district. Granted these maybe be false memories, but does it make them less real? Fill me up with disgust and self-pity? No. Instead I chose to turn my weakness into a strength. You too, I think, have that kind of courage and grit. A certain swarthy *gravitas*, unlike some other men around here. *(Beat)* Your predecessor knew that quite well.

MAN: My...*predecessor*?

WOMAN: Let me tell you, this used to be one big happy family here before you arrived.

MAN: Whatever happened to him? My predecessor?

WOMAN: Maybe you'd like to join our happy American family? There are always openings.

MAN: You haven't answered my question.

*(*WOMAN *opens a bowling bag. Extracts a formaldehyde brain from inside)*

WOMAN: Can't tell from this, but your predecessor must have weighed nearly five hundred pounds when he came in here. Thought he'd eat the whole damn place up. Used to call him the Sidney Greenstreet of terrorism. On account of the way he carried his weight, manipulated things with his fat little fingers. *(She lifts the disembodied brain and stares at it as if it were a crystal ball.)* Cogito ergo sum. *(She kisses brain.)* I think therefore I am. But what if you think my thoughts? Does that mean I'm you? Or vice versa, *you* are *me*? *(She inhales deeply, sniffing food, then runs over to devour what's left.)* God! I've never been this ravenous in my life.

MAN: Or maybe you're just pregnant.

WOMAN: Are you insane?

MAN: That's why you're so hungry.

WOMAN: How do you know that?

MAN: *Cogito ergo sum.*

WOMAN: How the fuck do you know what's inside me?

MAN: You should've been more careful.

WOMAN: I never gave you permission to read my mind.

MAN: Soon everyone will know your secret.

WOMAN: You are crazy, aren't you?!

MAN: Shhh! Don't you move!

WOMAN: What do you think you're doing?

(MAN places his hand on WOMAN's stomach. And whimpers like a baby. As if speaking on behalf of the unborn fetus.)

WOMAN: Get away from me!

MAN: It wants to talk to you.

WOMAN: No...

MAN: We might not know who's guilty here, but we all know who's the victim.

WOMAN: Get away from me!

MAN: *(Small voice, tender)* I love you Mommy. *(Wails like a newborn) I love you!*

WOMAN: No!

MAN: Don't abort me. I love you. *Waaah! Waah!*

(RON and DON run in.)

DON: You okay?

RON: We heard crying.

WOMAN: *(Covering up)* Everything's fine. Everything's just fine.

(Lights shift.)

Scene 15

(WOMAN stumbles around stage, makes sure she's alone, maybe humming a lullaby, then talking to the baby inside her.)

WOMAN: Can you feel this little one? Can you feel me touching you? If only I could hold and touch you rather than just carry you around inside me. Where are you? Can you hear me? Feel me? Like my thoughts you are part of me but you are not me. Here. *(She opens her mouth wide.)* Look at the world. Look out of my mouth and make sure you like what you see. Because once you come out there's no turning back. More light? Wider? Is this wide enough for you?

(She stands with her mouth wide open. In a spot of light. Just as—voice of PRESIDENT comes on.)

PRESIDENT: Dear America,

WOMAN: Shhh! The President is talking. Can you hear him Little One? *(All excited)* The Voice of our President...!! He's going to tell you a bedtime story. What a treat! Not every day you get to hear a bed time story from the mouth of the President. *(Resumes her pose, mouth open to light)*

PRESIDENT: Dear America,
As I (or one of my many doubles) reach out to you from my secret but constantly shifting hideout, one by one our Nation's proud monuments are being destroyed. First the Jefferson memorial, then the Lincoln. And last week, only last week, our sacred lady of diversity—the Statue of Liberty.

WOMAN: Is he scaring you? I'm sorry. Is the big bad President giving you nightmares?

PRESIDENT: I'd be lying if I said this campaign of terror isn't taking its toll on me. Because it is. I've lost weight. My memory isn't what it used to be. And my thoughts no longer seem my own. But there are still things that stick with me no matter what.

WOMAN: Don't be afraid, Little One. I'll protect you. I'll even kill for you. That's what all good parents do, kill for their children. So the children can grow up to become strong and powerful... What do you want to be when you grow up? A fireman, policeman...or perhaps a magician?

PRESIDENT: *(Explosion through Radio.)* Where was I? Ah yes... My first encounter with magic that fine Saturday morning.

(Another distant explosion. MAN *slowly lifts his head.)*

WOMAN: You could also become the President you know. Someone has to. Although I'd prefer magician... a magician can turn himself into many things, including the President.

PRESIDENT: It was my fifth birthday. And a young boy, not much older than me, was pulling a rabbit from a hat. But the rabbit, as it turned out, was dead. Most likely poisoned. And I didn't know who to feel worse for—the rabbit or the young magician. But I knew I never wanted to feel that way again. That kind of... awkwardness, it stays with you forever...

WOMAN: But what if I love you and lose you like everything else in my life. What will become of me then, Little One? What will become of us?

(Another Explosion. Radio flickers with Lights. WOMAN *rocks and sings lullaby to baby.)*

(Unseen, DON comes in and sits in corner.)

(Larger explosion)

Scene 16

(DON alone on stage, meditating, clutching a photo to his chest. No MAN. No RON. WOMAN enters.)

WOMAN: Meditating...?

DON: Actually, this time I *am* praying.

WOMAN: Really. I thought...

DON: *(Overlapping)* I know. I'm praying for my son. Henry. *(Shows her Henry's photo.)* He's been missing since yesterday's bombing.

WOMAN: I'm sorry to hear that. Must be so hard being a parent. All that anxiety, the dread, crushing the heart like some invisible paper weight.

DON: *(Admiring photo)* Henry hated secrets. To him they were like lies. Poor boy even tattled on himself. *Daddy— that's what he called me, Daddy—don't be angry, Daddy, but I did this...I broke that.*

WOMAN: No matter what happens now. He knew how much you loved him. You were his...confessor.

DON: Yes... but for some reason I still feel guilty. *(Sniffling)* And no matter how hard I try I can't stop thinking about that one time he hid himself behind the living room door waiting to surprise me. *(Pause)* I tell you, for someone who hated secrets as much as he did, he sure loved to hide behind doors and scare people— *boo!* —even though I warned him that it made Daddy very tense and nervous. *(Pause)* So one day—I don't know what got into me—but one day I decided to teach him a lesson and I just kicked the door open, knowing full well he was hiding behind it. Blood everywhere. He sure learned his lesson. But now it makes me sad just to think about it.

WOMAN: And that makes you want to pray?

DON: It's better than crying. Think they'll find him? *(He regards Henry's photo one more time.)* Look at those eyes. That sweet soulful look. If anything could make you believe in God it'd be the innocence in those eyes.

WOMAN: *(Also looking)* I hate to say this, especially at a time like this and all, but have you ever seen Hitler's baby picture...? Same sweet look in his eyes.

DON: *(Snatches back photo)* My son's not going to become another Hitler.

WOMAN: I'm sure you're right, but life is always so full of surprises.

DON: No.

WOMAN: Maybe that's why he died.

DON: They might still find him! He might still be alive.

WOMAN: Of course, of course. There's always hope... before death. But knowing what you do now, you think you could've murdered the baby Hitler in his crib.

DON: My son is alive!

WOMAN: I mean Nazis aren't so bad anymore. Not with all those nouveau riche terrorists on the block. *(Re: photo)* Wow, what's this?

DON: *(Angry)* Just some dirt or something.

WOMAN: I don't think so.

DON: A smudge...

WOMAN: No...this! Is this a mustache? You draw this on your own son's picture?

DON: *(Also looking)* What are you talking about?
I never saw this before.

WOMAN: Hitler baby.

DON: Stop!

WOMAN: How did the mustache get there? *(Wry)*
Just grew by itself, I suppose.

DON: I don't know. Maybe Ron.

WOMAN: Or our guest. That's the thing about magic,
you're always trying to figure out...*how*? How did they
do that? *(She suddenly doubles over.)* Oh my God!

DON: What's wrong?

WOMAN: *(Massaging stomach)* Nothing. Just some pain.
Nothing to concern you. *(She prepares to exit.)* You just
go on and pray if you can. I won't bother you any
longer.

DON: You can stay if you want.

WOMAN: Do I have to pray?

DON: If you want. From above, on our knees, we all
look the same when we pray. Facing Mecca with our
backs to Jerusalem, or facing Jerusalem with our backs
to Mecca—it's all the same from above.

WOMAN: What would I pray for?

DON: That's between you and God.

WOMAN: My little *secret*, eh?

DON: After all, he *is* supposed to be the best mindreader
around.

WOMAN: God...?

DON: If you believe in him, yeah, he'll read everything
in your heart before the words can even touch it.

(DON *begins to prays.* WOMAN *joins him. They pray together. All at once*—WOMAN *bends over and starts throwing up.)*

DON: If it's going to make you sick. Don't do it.

WOMAN: It's not the prayer.

DON: What is it then?

WOMAN: My...secret.

(Lights out)

Scene 17

(RON *fiddles with radio, it goes in and out.* DON *regards his efforts with bemusement.)*

PRESIDENT: And where is the President secreted today? From what new and undisclosed location is his Voice talking to you now? What corner of his head is all this crap coming from? Ooooo...*I spy the President!* Is he is in the *White House*? Or is it the *Rose Garden*? The *Pentagon*? *Camp David...*? Or perhaps he's just wandering about lost in the stormy jungle of his wits

(DON starts laughing.)

RON: What's so funny?

DON: I was just thinking about the President.

RON: That's funny...?

DON: No, but did you know that whenever the President travels, he makes sure to bring his own personal bomb along.

RON: Is this a joke?

DON: So finally, one day, they stop him at the airport and ask: Mister President. Why the bomb? Obviously you are *not* a terrorist, so why the bomb? To which the

President replies: I always carry a bomb because the odds of there being *two* bombs on any one flight are much smaller than one.

(DON *laughs.* RON *is straight-faced.*)

RON: *(Humorless)* I don't get it.

(MAN *also laughs.*)

DON: *(Taunting) He* gets it!

(MAN *laughs even louder.*)

RON: *So fuckin what!* He gets it. Big fuckin deal! I'm tired of his bullshit. *(Beat)* Know what I'm gonna do, Don, I'm gonna think out of the box for once. That's right, I'm gonna think out of the box by getting *inside* his box.

DON: *(Chuckling)* You going to rape him again?

RON: No. I'm gonna go in there and read his mind for a change.

DON: Since when can you read minds?

RON: Can't be that hard. I mean look at this guy. He can do it, so can I. I'm gonna uncover the real dirt beneath his nails, under his skull... *(He places his hand against* MAN'*s forehead.)*

DON: You hear that, buddy? This is your last chance. *(To* RON*)* Well...? What's taking so long? What's going on up there?

RON: *(Hand pressed to forehead)* I'm just preheating the oven.

DON: Here, try this. *(He hands* RON *the* MAN'*s turban.)* Maybe this will give you an edge.

(RON *puts it on.)*

RON: How do I look?

DON: Very authentic.

(Again RON *touches* MAN's *head, concentrates.)*

RON: *(Pleased)* I think it's starting to work.

DON: Just tell us what you see.

RON: *(Very theatrical)* Open sesame! Yes. I'm starting to get something now...I'm just not sure if they're his thoughts or mine.

DON: *(Overeager)* What? What is it? What do you see?

RON: Oh my god. Oh my god!

DON: Something to do with China...isn't it? China or North Korea...?

RON: This is much worse than I feared.

DON: It's the president. Isn't it? It's him.

(MAN remains quiet, says nothing throughout.)

RON: Much...much worse.

DON: What about him? What about the president?

RON: *(Portentous, trance-like)* Beware Mister President, beware! *(He collapses.)*

(Lights out)

Scene 18

(RON, DON, and WOMAN are huddled around radio, listening intently. MAN is apart, as if stranded on his own island.)

RADIO—PRESIDENT: My dear fellow Americans, I am speaking to you from a strange, undisclosed location in your *past* to assure you that soon the terror will end and freedom will again be restored to the open American skies. Today the world will note that the first atomic bomb was dropped on Hiroshima, a military base.

WOMAN: Did he say Atomic Bomb?

DON: Hiroshima?

WOMAN: *(To* DON*)* I thought you said you got the radio fixed.

DON: *(Disapproval)* Ron...?

RON: I did. I swear I did.

(RON *fiddles with radio. No help)*

PRESIDENT: We wished in this first attack to avoid, insofar as possible, the killing of civilians. But that attack is only a warning of things to come.

RON: Maybe it's the History Channel.

DON: On the radio?

WOMAN: I was worried about this.

DON: About what...?

WOMAN: This is much worse than I suspected.

RON: What's worse?

WOMAN: I don't even like to say this, but I think the President has... *(Pointed whisper)* ...lost his mind.

DON: You sure it's the President.

WOMAN: It's not Harry S Truman.

PRESIDENT:...If Japan does not surrender, bombs will have to be dropped on her war industries and, unfortunately, thousands of civilian lives will be lost.

WOMAN: I'm sad to say boys, but I think this marks the end of the American Empire. The halcyon days of American ascendancy are over.

DON: *(To* RON*)* Is this what you saw when you read his mind earlier?

RON: I don't remember.

DON: Of course not.

WOMAN: All those explosions must've taken their toll on our poor President. His sovereign mind blanked out like an etch-a-sketch shook by an angry child.

PRESIDENT: *(Ongoing in background)* To prevent our demise we must look in the mirror of History where the guillotine is sharpened daily to keep freedom alive.

WOMAN: Turn that thing off!!

PRESIDENT: *(Portentous)* A new Rein of Terror must replace the old Rein of Terror. And...

WOMAN: *(Over radio)* I said off!! Turn that shit off now!!

RON: Okay, okay. I'm trying.

WOMAN: *And don't ever turn it back on without my permission!*

(Radio finally goes off. Beat)

RON: *(Whispering to* DON*)* What's up with her?

DON: *(Sotto voce)* Don't know. But she look bigger to you?

(They stare at WOMAN *who's beginning to visibly show.)*

WOMAN: What?! What are you staring at?!

(Silence. More distant explosions)

DON: So what do we do now?

WOMAN: Now?

DON: Now that the President is Missing In Action, so to speak, who will lead us now?

RON: Tell us what to do...

WOMAN: We do the same things as before.

RON: But...

WOMAN: We ask questions.

DON: More questions?

WOMAN: If anyone knows what's inside the President's mind, it's him.

RON: But what if he won't tell us?

WOMAN: He'll have to. Won't you? Won't you?!

(MAN *says nothing.*)

DON: You really think he knows?

WOMAN: Look at him smiling. Of course he knows. With that *smile*. Besides, he's our only chance. The only one who can help us make a difference between containment and catastrophe.

(*Suddenly*—WOMAN *gets to her knees before* MAN.)

WOMAN: All Hail to the new Chief!

(DON *joins her in genuflection.*)

DON: Hail to the New Chief!

(RON *is hesitant to join them, watches resentfully.*)

WOMAN: (*Meaning* RON) Don!

DON: I'm Don.

WOMAN: Of course you are. (*Sharp admonishment*) Ron!

DON: Ron...

(RON *finally genuflects to* MAN.)

RON: (*Reluctantly*) All Hail the Chief.

WOMAN: Speak to us new Chief. What does the President say? Speak to us Mister President.

(MAN *lays his hands on the radio—as if channeling it. Then opens his mouth. Static issues forth. Like a radio being tuned in and out of bad reception.*)

(*Lights out.*)

Scene 19

(MAN sits hugging radio. He keeps tuning the dial to get reception. At first more static, as if carried over from previous scene, then some words. He seems to be mouthing the words—but we are not sure if they are his words or he is ventriloquizing.)

RADIO—MAN: Testing one-two-three testing. *(More static)* Is anyone there? This is the Voice of your... *(Clears his throat)* ...President speaking. *(More static)* Hello? Is anyone out there? Hello...? *(Adjusting dial more carefully)* I am here. *(Listens)* Good. Always here. Very good. *(Pause)* Nowhere to hide. Not even in the shadow of my own thoughts. To be always found out. Exposed. Is this my end? My finish...? Where I wave goodbye to the fear of all that we don't know. Fear of intimacy... of ourselves...of intimacy *with* ourselves...
And yet in my dreams I am a child. Playing hide and seek. Invisible but in plain sight. Screaming *"Here I am! Right over here!"* But nobody comes to get me. I am alone. Unseen, unheard. Like I was living in someone else's dream.
And when I wake up from this desolate graveyard of undreamt dreams, nothing remains of me. Not even the promise of my words. Nothing.
I don't want to get too philosophical here, after all I am just the... *(Coughs)* ...President—but I do feel like I have awakened from another time, jetlagged from living in another person's dream... Whose dream I'm not sure. But I know it's not mine.

(Another explosion. Beat)

(MAN rises slowly. Tentatively. Looks around. Puts radio down on chair and prepares to leave.)

(But an invisible voice barks at him to stay still.)

RON: Sit crusader!

DON: We're still here. Infidel.

RON: Surprise!

DON: But now we're invisible, imperialist.

RON: That's real magic, baby.

DON: Like the thoughts parading inside your head.
We're here. But you can't see us.

RON: Over here.

DON: Just follow our voice. Use our voice to guide your
eyes.

(Slowly, concealed from head to toe in similar burkas—
RON *and* DON *materialize from opposite corners of the
room—now turning away from the curtains against which
they've been standing, camouflaged by their burkas.)*

DON: Here we are!

RON: Right over here, Mister President.

DON: Secreted beneath our clothes we are now
interchangeable to your eyes.

(They advance threateningly towards MAN. *Ululating
in high pitched voices. It is difficult to tell who is who as
they converge upon him, the dark folds of their burkas
gesticulating in air, undulating in the slow breeze of their
arms.)*

MAN: Leave me alone. Get away from me! Get away!

*(*MAN *tries to protest—as* DON *and* RON *knot a blindfold
around his eyes.)*

DON: So interesting, Don, the way the enemy you
can't see becomes the enemy inside you. Internalized,
interiorized. Something you can never escape. Avoid.

RON: *(Puzzling this out)* You mean Ron.

DON: Excuse me...?

RON: *(Peeking under burka)* You called me Don. I'm Ron. You're Don.

DON: I am?

RON: Does it matter?

DON: Not to me.

RON: Me neither.

DON: *(To* MAN*)* How about you? Does it Matter to you Mister President?

RON: Oh Yoohoo! Mister President, over here. Over here!

*(*MAN *wanders about room in a parody of Blind Man's Bluff.* RON *and* DON *just out of reach as he repeatedly lunges, trying to grab them.)*

DON: No. Over here. Right here!

RON: Come and get it!

DON: Oh! So close.

RON: ... and yet so far.

DON: Come. We're here to...give you a helping hand.

RON: All you have to do is take it.

*(*DON *offers his hand, but retracts it last minute.* MAN *lunges, misses. Falls to the ground)*

DON: On your knees. *Now!*

RON: *(Shoving him into floor)* You heard the man.

DON: Pray to your God and reveal to him what you won't tell us. You do believe in God don't you?

RON: *(To* DON*)* Christ! How many times are you going to ask him that?!

DON: Until I get the right answer. *(To* MAN*) Pray!*

RON: That can take all night.

DON: Before he gets anointed.

(MAN *is silent.*)

DON: Louder! Maybe God can hear you, but we sure as hell can't. Go on. If not for yourself, pray for your sister. Let's hear the clairvoyant prayer issuing forth from that tight and genuflected space you call your heart.

(*Blindfolded* MAN *rises and stumbles to window. Radio in hand. Then throws radio out*)

MAN: *No!*

DON: You say something Don?

RON: I told you I'm not Don!

DON: Sorry, Ron. Did you hear something?

RON: Nothing, Don. Nothing.

MAN: *(Beat)* You want me to pray but you have no intention of listening to what I have to say....

DON: You think it's any different with God?

RON: I told you he was an ungrateful piece of shit.

WOMAN: *(Entering)* America is waiting Mister President.

(RON *angrily trips* MAN—*who collides with* WOMAN *as she enters with scalding coffee. It spills all over* MAN.)

WOMAN: Oh shit! You okay?

(MAN *howls in pain.* WOMAN *helps him up. Notes* RON *and* DON *in their matching burkas.*)

WOMAN: Ron...what the hell's going on here?

RON: How did she know it was me?

DON: It was all his idea. I swear!

WOMAN: You should treat the President with more respect.

RON: But how did you know. Under all this. How could you tell it was me?

WOMAN: *(Pointing at* DON*'s burka)* Cause he's Don. Stupid.

(Black out)

Scene 20

*(*WOMAN *is noticeably pregnant.* MAN *has hood over his head.)*

WOMAN: I remember thinking my whole life that if I could perform just one trick and do it well, I'd be perfectly happy. Create one illusion on which to base all my other delusions. Well, I've been perfecting my one trick and I'm almost there. *(Polishing her belly)* Should I tell you what it is...this trick...? ...Or just let you guess?

*(*WOMAN *goes into some rhythmic breathing ritual.)*

WOMAN: But look at you standing there—cold and shivering—while I can't stop talking. *(She leads him by the hand.)* Come Mister President. You must get ready. Your audience is waiting. Time to air out your secret once and for all. *(She positions* MAN*'s head to stare out window.)* Time to look outside at the injured world and tell them what you see. What you've destroyed.

*(*MAN *begins to remove his hood.* WOMAN *stops him.)*

WOMAN: No. You leave that on Mister President. Narrate the tragedy with your heart. Not your eyes.

(As MAN *begins to talk,* WOMAN*'s breath quickens.)*

MAN: Before me I see the world as it must have been ages ago.

*(*WOMAN *breathes faster and faster.)*

MAN: Untouched by the light of human eyes.

WOMAN: Go on.

MAN: A time before Presidents roamed the earth.

(WOMAN *begins to hyperventilate.*)

WOMAN: Oh my God! It's happening. Ron, Don. Someone. Quick. The magic is about to happen.

(RON *and* DON *rush in wearing medical scrubs. Masks across their face. Again it is difficult to tell them apart.*

(WOMAN *begins to go into labor, right then and there.*)

RON: I told you she looked fat.

DON: What do you want us to do?

RON: I'll hold her legs.

DON: I've got her head.

(*As* MAN *narrates the vision of his hooded eyes—* WOMAN *gives birth, assisted by* RON *and* DON.)

(*In the near distance a set of muffled explosions, always coming closer.*)

MAN: (*Calmly*) Outside I see a world without the trace of a blueprint—unscratched and pristine—before the buildings that have now fallen had ever been built or even dreamed of.

RON: (*Re: childbirth*) I can see the head.

DON: Keep breathing.

RON: I can see the fuckin head.

MAN: (*Narrative*) And above the humble ruins of these once-erect edifices I now see a flock of black birds, like cinders, writing their careless little secret across a new horizon with the thin edge of their wings. A horizon whose simple and uninterrupted beauty is like a blank page in mankind's history.

WOMAN: *(Grunting)* Is it here? Am I done? Is it here?

MAN: And yet looking out at the meager leftovers of our once glorious city, I've often thought about that first time magic came into existence. Not my first time, mind you. But that first *first* time magic was ever discovered. First by accident. Then by design. Like some scientific experiment we take for granted. Or like Democracy. Yes. The unspoken magic of democracy at work building new nations all around us...

(DON holds up the newborn.)

(MAN removes his hood.)

RON: Oh my God, Your baby is here. It's here.

DON: Look at those eyes!

WOMAN: Let me see the little angel.

DON: The haunting innocence in those eyes!

(They hand her the baby. RON leads MAN to coffin.)

MAN: I wasn't born the President...you know, I was *made* into one...

WOMAN: *(Cooing)* Momma's here. Momma loves you.

MAN: Where else could I have been fed and loved against my will? Where else but in a democracy can you have someone rise through ranks the way I did, from the lowest to the highest. *(He stares into video and addresses the unseen masses.)* But now, dear Citzens, now that I *am* your adopted President (and you are my adopted country) not even death will take me away from you or your sweet memory. I will be remembered forever in the smiles of children. And children of all ages and sex will be named after me....

WOMAN: *(Tender to violent)* Who loves you... who loves you? *Who loves you for chrissakes!!!*

MAN: There's a love I have for my country. An inarticulate love that here at this moment brings forth tears of joy from my heart and bears the name of...*sacrifice*. [Sobs louder] So that now as President I've already forgotten my old self and suffering— so I can concentrate only on *you*, my children. God Bless America! And good night.

WOMAN: Why won't it cry?

DON: *(Shrugs)* It's smiling.

WOMAN: Why is it so quiet?

RON: It's got his fuckin smile.

WOMAN: Make the little angel cry!! Make it cry!!

(RON *and* DON *demur, wanting nothing to do with it.* WOMAN *offers newborn to* MAN.)

WOMAN: Here. For you. This is my *gift* to you, Mister President.

MAN: What do you want me to do with it?

WOMAN: Take it. Watch it grow. Study the way it sits, stands, walks...and *smiles*. Five minutes with a newborn and right away you realize all the things we take for granted. The time-lapse *magic* of our day-to-day life. Think about it. The only thing we know from birth, on our own, is how to cry. And mine never even did that.

MAN: Your baby is...dead.

WOMAN: Whose fault is that?

MAN: Still-born to be precise.

WOMAN: I just want it to cry.

MAN: As President I offer you my deepest condolences for this regrettable loss of human life

WOMAN: Please make it cry!

PRESIDENT:But sometimes sacrifices must be made.

WOMAN: Can't you make it cry?

MAN: Perhaps it's time you bury it?

WOMAN: Like your secret...?

MAN: What secret is that?

WOMAN: You tell us.

MAN: I already have.

DON: *Tell us again!*

RON: *Now!*

MAN: Tool late for that, I'm afraid.

(A final and loud explosion rocks room.)

(When smoke clears, MAN has magically disappeared.)

(Baby is left on floor.)

DON: Where did he go?

(Baby finally starts to cry.)

WOMAN: Did you hear that? *(More crying)* Did you all hear that?

RON: Just another one of his tricks.

DON: Like my son, our President has vanished....

WOMAN: Someone pick it up.

RON: Did he jump out the window?

DON: First my son, now the President.

WOMAN: Pick it up, for Chrissake! *(Joyful)* It's crying. It's crying!!

(DON lifts the baby.)

DON: Call it Henry. Can we. Call it that?

RON: Where the fuck did he go?

WOMAN: First stop the crying.

RON: I thought you wanted it to cry.

WOMAN: I did. And now I want it to stop.

(Baby cries louder.)

RON: We'll need another President, you know.

DON: What about the name Henry?

WOMAN: Sure. Henry. Why not. But first make it stop!

(Baby cries as lights fade.)

END OF PLAY